D1709049

ACTION SPORTS

BIG AIR SKATEBOARDING

By K. A. Hale

Kaleidoscope

Minneapolis, MN

BIGFOOT BOOKS

The Quest for Discovery Never Ends

This edition is co-published by agreement between Kaleidoscope and World Book, Inc.

Kaleidoscope Publishing, Inc.
6012 Blue Circle Drive
Minnetonka, MN 55343 U.S.A.

World Book, Inc.
180 North LaSalle St., Suite 900
Chicago IL 60601 U.S.A.

Kaleidoscope ISBNs
978-1-64519-063-9 (library bound)
978-1-64494-144-7 (paperback)
978-1-64519-164-3 (ebook)

World Book ISBN
978-0-7166-4356-2 (library bound)

Library of Congress Control Number
2019938875

Printed in the United States of America.

FIND ME
IF YOU CAN!

Bigfoot lurks within one of the images in this book. It's up to you to find him!

TABLE OF
CONTENTS

Chapter 1: *Going for Gold*.. 4

Chapter 2: *The Birth of Big Air* 10

Chapter 3: *Ramps, Boards, and Gear* 16

Chapter 4: *Big Names in Big Air* 22

Beyond the Book.. 28

Research Ninja.. 29

Further Resources 30

Glossary 31

Index 32

Photo Credits.. 32

About the Author... 32

GOING FOR GOLD

It's July 21, 2018. Mitchie Brusco stands at the top of the MegaRamp. It's inside a stadium. The enormous ramp is 73.5 feet (22.4 m) tall. Brusco is twenty-one years old. He's competing in the X Games Skateboard Big Air Final. He will skate down the ramp. Then he will jump over a 50-foot (15 m) gap. Next, he will do a trick off the **quarterpipe**. He has five tries to get the highest score. He's tried three times. But he hasn't landed his quarterpipe trick. He's in ninth place.

Mitchie Brusco competed on a MegaRamp set up for the X Games at US Bank Stadium in Minneapolis, Minnesota.

Big air skateboarding is a dangerous sport. Skaters fall a lot. Brusco fell on all three of his runs so far. Earlier, one skater fell and hurt his stomach. Another got hit in the face by his skateboard. Brusco wears a helmet, knee pads, and elbow pads. They help keep him from getting hurt. But he doesn't think too much about the danger. Doing cool tricks is more important to him.

Brusco moves his skateboard to the edge. He steps on it to tilt down. Then, he zooms down the ramp. He **launches** off the middle ramp. He does a trick over the gap. He starts with his left foot back. He makes the board flip under his feet. He spins halfway. His left foot ends forward. He lands it. But he can't celebrate yet. He still has the quarterpipe.

He's going to try a **1080**. Another skater had landed a 1080 first. But Brusco was the first to do it at the X Games. He did it in Barcelona five years ago. But he hasn't tried since then.

DEGREES

The numbers in the names of tricks are called degrees. A 360 is 360 degrees. It is the same as one full turn. A 180 is half of a turn. A 1080, or 1080 degrees, is three full turns. Only a few skaters can land a 1080.

Because big air skateboarders get so high up, they're more likely to get hurt if they fall.

Mitchie Brusco won a gold medal for Skateboard Big Air at the 2018 X Games.

He builds up speed. He flies off the quarterpipe. He grabs his board as he spins. He spins once, then twice. He spins a third time. He lands! The crowd goes wild. He landed a 1080. He can't believe it. He sits at the bottom of the ramp in shock. Another skater helps him up and gives him a hug. He goes to the side of the ramp. He waits for his score. He earns a ninety-two. Now he is in first place! There are other skaters who go after him. But no one can beat him. Mitchie Brusco wins his first X Games gold medal.

CHAPTER 2

THE BIRTH OF BIG AIR

Big air skateboarding exists thanks to Mat Hoffman. Hoffman is a **BMX** pro rider. He made the first "big air" ramp in 1992. It was 20 feet (6 m) tall. He needed help getting up to speed. He had to go fast to get up the ramp. A motorcycle **towed** him on his bike.

FUN FACT
BMX Big Air has been part of the X Games since 2006.

The first big air ramp came from the world of BMX.

Hoffman's BMX ramp led to a halfpipe where riders performed tricks.

Hoffman built a second ramp a few years later. This one had a **roll-in**. He could use it to build up speed. Now he wouldn't need the motorcycle. The roll-in led to a **halfpipe**.

HISTORY OF SKATEBOARDING

The earliest skateboards looked different from ones today. They were made from boards with roller skates attached. Surfers used them in the 1950s for "sidewalk surfing." They did this when the waves were low. Better wheels were invented in the 1970s. They let skateboarders do more tricks.

RECORDS IN BIG AIR

SKATEBOARDING

Most X Games gold medals in Skateboard Big Air

Bob Burnquist   8 medals

Highest air on a skateboard (quarterpipe)

Danny Way   25.49 ft (7.77 m)

Longest skateboard ramp jump

Danny Way   79 ft (24 m) (on a MegaRamp)

First skateboarder to land a 1080

Tom Schaar   March 26, 2012

Skateboarder Danny Way heard about Hoffman's ramp. He was inspired by it. Way wondered if he could make something like it for skateboarding. He created the first MegaRamp in 2002. It had a roll-in like Hoffman's. But the rest was different. Way put a gap in the middle. Skaters would have to jump over it. After the gap, there was a quarterpipe. Way's ramp was long. He could do tricks much higher in the air. The MegaRamp came to the X Games in 2004. Big air skateboarding was born.

The MegaRamp allows skaters to go faster and fly higher.

CHAPTER 3

The MegaRamp's roll-in starts very high up so that skaters can get up to speed before jumping over the gap.

RAMPS, BOARDS, AND GEAR

Carlos stands at the top of the MegaRamp. He blocks the sun from his eyes. He looks at the ramp. It's huge. He is at Woodward West. This skate park is in California. There is a permanent MegaRamp here. It's one of only two in the world. The other one is at Bob Burnquist's house. That one is called Dreamland. Dreamland isn't open to the public.

A MegaRamp has three parts. There is a roll-in to gain speed. Then there is a gap up to 70 feet (21 m) wide. At Woodward West, he can choose his gap size. It's 50 feet (15 m), 60 feet (18 m), or 70 feet (21 m). Across the gap sits a tall quarterpipe. The ramp has a smooth wood surface.

Skaters wear helmets, kneepads, elbow pads, and other padding to help protect themselves.

27-foot (8 m) quarterpipe

Skaters wear helmets and knee pads. These keep them safe. Carlos also wears pads on his back and elbows. He has duct tape over his shoelaces. This keeps them from shredding if he falls.

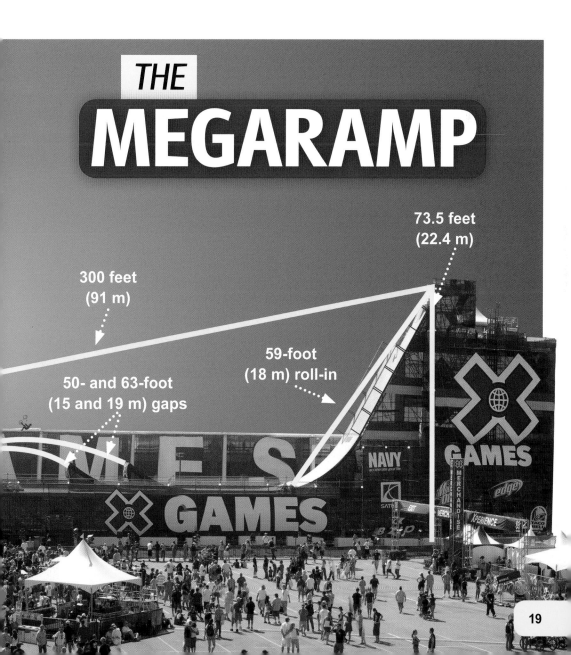

THE

MEGARAMP

73.5 feet
(22.4 m)

300 feet
(91 m)

59-foot
(18 m) roll-in

50- and 63-foot
(15 and 19 m) gaps

Skateboarders can design their own skateboards. They choose the deck. The deck is the flat part they stand on. They can choose what is printed on the bottom. Then they choose the **trucks** and wheels. Carlos and his friends all have different boards. His deck has a dragon on it. His wheels are bright green. He likes that his board is unique.

Carlos skates down the roll-in. He builds up speed. He flies off the ramp! He reaches the other side. But he loses his balance. He falls off his board. He slides down on his knees. The pads keep him from getting hurt. He gets up to try again.

Skateboards can be personalized with unique deck designs, wheel colors, and other custom features.

CHAPTER 4

BIG NAMES IN BIG AIR

The X Games is a competition for **extreme sports**. It hosts the only major big air skateboarding competition. Some of the best athletes in the world compete.

Danny Way started the big air skateboarding movement. He brought the MegaRamp to the X Games in 2004. Way was a big dreamer. He wanted to do something special. In 2005, he used a MegaRamp to jump over the Great Wall of China. The section he jumped over was originally 70 feet (21 m) wide. But he did a practice run. He fell and hurt his ankle. His sponsors were mad. They said the gap needed to be shorter. A construction team worked on the ramp overnight. They shortened the gap by 10 feet (3 m). The next day, Way made the jump.

THE X GAMES

The X Games started in 1995. There are different sports in the winter and the summer. The summer games include skateboarding, motocross, and BMX. The winter sports include skiing and snowboarding. Skateboard Big Air has been part of the X Games since 2004.

Danny Way famously used a MegaRamp to jump over the Great Wall of China.

Bob Burnquist's yard has one of only two permanent MegaRamps in the world.

FUN FACT
Burnquist went pro at age fourteen.

Bob Burnquist competed in the first X Games in 1995. He competed in every summer X Games until 2017. He was the only person to compete in every one. He started out with **vert skateboarding**. Later on, he tried big air. In 1999, he bought a farm. It was near San Diego, California. He built a skateboard pool in the front yard.

He built a corkscrew ramp. In 2006, he did something big. He built the first permanent MegaRamp in the world. This gave him and other skaters a place to practice. His skate park is called Dreamland. Lots of professional skaters practice at Dreamland.

Tom Schaar was twelve years old when he made history. It was March 26, 2012. Schaar landed the first-ever skateboarding 1080. Shaun White and Mitchie Brusco were both trying to do one. People thought one of them would be first. Schaar surprised them all. He was practicing at Woodward West. He decided to try a 1080 for the first time that day. First, he warmed up with some smaller tricks. Then, he tried the 1080. He did it four times without landing. Finally, on his fifth try, he landed! He said, "It was the hardest trick I've ever done. But it was easier than I thought."

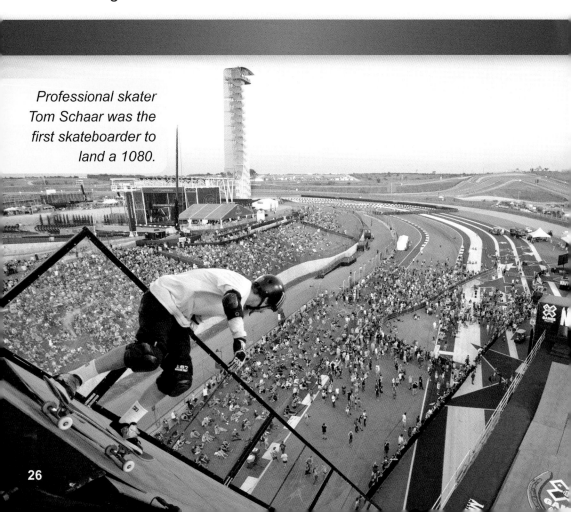

Professional skater Tom Schaar was the first skateboarder to land a 1080.

SKATEBOARDING

DANNY WAY

Danny Way made the first MegaRamp for skateboards in 2002. He jumped over the Great Wall of China in 2005. He did it live on Chinese television. Twenty-five million people watched.

BOB BURNQUIST

Brazilian American skater Bob Burnquist has earned more X Games medals than anyone in history. He has eight gold medals in Skateboard Big Air. He built the first permanent MegaRamp in his backyard near San Diego, California.

TOM SCHAAR

Tom Schaar was the first skateboarder ever to land a 1080. He did it in March 2012. He was in the X Games for the first time that same year. He was twelve. In 2014, he won a gold medal in Skateboard Big Air. He became the youngest big air medalist in history.

THE BOOK

After reading the book, it's time to think about what you learned.
Try the following exercises to jumpstart your ideas.

THINK

THAT'S NEWS TO ME. Think about when Danny Way jumped the Great Wall of China. How would news sources give you more details about the jump? What information could you find in a news article? Where could you go to look for those news sources?

CREATE

PRIMARY SOURCES. Primary sources are documents or sources that were made at the time of an event. Photographs, videos, and interviews are all examples of primary sources. Make a list of primary sources you could use to find out more about Big Air Skateboarding.

SHARE

SUM IT UP. Write one paragraph summarizing the important points of the book. Remember to use your own words, not just copy things down. Share your paragraph with a classmate. What do they think of your summary? Do they have questions you can answer?

GROW

REAL-LIFE RESEARCH. Think about some real-world places you could go to learn more about Big Air Skateboarding. What kinds of things would you learn at these places? Who could you talk to at these places to learn more?

RESEARCH NINJA

Visit *www.ninjaresearcher.com/0639* to learn how
to take your research skills and book report writing to the next level!

RESEARCH

DIGITAL LITERACY TOOLS

SEARCH LIKE A PRO
Learn about how to use search engines to find useful websites.

FACT OR FAKE?
Discover how you can tell a trusted website from an untrustworthy resource.

TEXT DETECTIVE
Explore how to zero in on the information you need most.

SHOW YOUR WORK
Research responsibly—learn how to cite sources.

WRITE

GET TO THE POINT
Learn how to express your main ideas.

PLAN OF ATTACK
Learn prewriting exercises and create an outline.

DOWNLOADABLE REPORT FORMS

FURTHER RESOURCES

BOOKS

Abdo, Kenny. *Skateboarding*. Abdo Publishing, 2018.

Adamson, Thomas K. *Big Air Skateboarding*. Bellwether Media, 2016.

Loh-Hagan, Virginia. *Extreme Skateboarding*. 45th Parallel Press, 2016.

WEBSITES

Factsurfer.com gives you a safe, fun way to find more information.

1. Go to www.factsurfer.com.

2. Enter "Big Air Skateboarding" into the search box and click 🔍.

3. Select your book cover to see a list of related websites.

GLOSSARY

1080: A 1080 is a 1080-degree turn, or three full turns in the air. Mitchie Brusco landed a 1080 in the 2018 X Games.

BMX: BMX stands for bicycle motocross. BMX riders race on tracks with ramps or do tricks in the air.

extreme sports: Extreme sports are sports that are considered more dangerous than others. The X Games hosts competitions for a number of exciting extreme sports.

halfpipe: A halfpipe is a ramp that's shaped like the letter *U*. Mat Hoffman's second big ramp was a halfpipe with a roll-in.

launches: When someone launches, they take off at great speed. A skater launches off the MegaRamp.

quarterpipe: A quarterpipe is a ramp that's shaped like half of the letter *U*. The MegaRamp ends in a quarterpipe where skaters do tricks.

roll-in: A roll-in is a big ramp to skate or ride down and build up speed. The roll-in lets skaters go very fast so they can jump over the gap.

towed: To be towed is to be pulled behind something else. Mat Hoffman was towed behind a motorcycle to get up to speed on his bike.

trucks: Trucks are the part of a skateboard the wheels go on. A skateboarder uses the trucks to steer.

vert skateboarding: Vert skateboarding is short for vertical skateboarding. In vert skateboarding, skaters use a quarterpipe or halfpipe to perform tricks.

INDEX

1080, 6, 9, 14, 26, 27

BMX, 10, 22
Brusco, Mitchie, 4–6, 9, 26
Burnquist, Bob, 14, 17, 24–25, 27

degrees, 6
Dreamland, 17, 25

halfpipes, 13
Hoffman, Mat, 10, 13, 15

MegaRamp, 4, 14, 15, 17–19, 22, 25, 27

quarterpipes, 4, 6, 9, 14, 15, 18

records, 14
roll-ins, 13, 15, 18, 19, 21

safety gear, 5, 19
Schaar, Tom, 14, 26, 27
skateboards, 13, 20

tricks, 4–6, 13, 15, 26

vert skateboarding, 24

Way, Danny, 14, 15, 22, 23, 27
White, Shaun, 26
Woodward West, 17–18, 26

X Games, 4, 6, 9, 10, 14, 15, 22, 24, 27

PHOTO CREDITS

The images in this book are reproduced through the courtesy of: Branimir Kvartuc/AP Images, front cover (skater); freelanceartist/Shutterstock Images, front cover (background); A. Einsiedler/ Shutterstock Images, front cover (ramp); Dynamicfoto-PedroCampos/iStockphoto, p. 3; David Berding/Icon Sportswire, pp. 4–5; A.Ricardo/Shutterstock Images, pp. 6–7, 15; Sean M. Haffey/Getty Images Sport/Getty Images, pp. 8–9; Kathy Hutchins/Shutterstock Images, p. 9; Tinseltown/Shutterstock Images, pp. 10, 27 (top); Raphael Daniaud/Shutterstock Images, pp. 10–11; Susana Luzir/Shutterstock Images, p. 12; underworld111/iStockphoto, p. 13; Red Line Editorial, p. 14; Allen J. Schaben/Los Angeles Times/Getty Images, p. 16–17; hurricanehank/ Shutterstock Images, p. 17; afby71/iStockphoto, pp. 18, 30; Tony Donaldson/Icon Sportswire, pp. 18–19; FiledImage/Shutterstock Images, pp. 20–21; China Newsphoto/Reuters/Newscom, p. 23; Jay Janner/Austin American-Statesman/AP Images, pp. 24–25, 26; Nate Beckett/Splash News/Newscom, p. 27 (center); Peter West/ACE Pictures/Newscom, p. 27 (bottom).

ABOUT THE AUTHOR

K. A. Hale is a writer and editor from Minnesota. She enjoys reading, writing, and playing with her dog.